Dr. Melanie-Marie Haywood

The UK University guide: A pocketbook for Higher Education
Students of Colour

CONTENTS

To the beautiful Black woman she will be one day.
To the beautiful Black girl she is.
To the dream that this world will be ready for all her beauty.

Foreword

Ahead of you is a pocketbook that knows you: it knows your struggles, your hopes and dreams for your time at university. We – the Black and Brown faces who have navigated these whitewashed spaces – know all too well what you're going through because we've been there too. Are you exhausted? Angry? Disappointed? We feel you.

We have shared glances across seminar rooms, rolled our eyes in silent symphony, told stories to a clamouring 'same!' because these are the realities of our existence in places that weren't built for us. In fact, these places are the very product of colonialism, imperialism, enslavement, displacement and racialised violence. A centuries-long foundation that cannot be unwritten by a three-year equality, diversity and inclusion strategy.

Students of colour, past and present, are collegiate in their shared experience of the endless barriers presented by institutional racism, as it intertwines with classism, sexism, homophobia, transphobia, disablism and more. It's up to us to be more than siblings in struggle, to be even more collegiate in our shared survival, resistance and joy.

So, I urge you to share these affirmations with those around you. I hope they aid your collective survival, and that – together – you go on to create pockets of joy. Study together! Sing and dance together! Cook together! Forming communities in spaces designed to individualise is a revolutionary act.

Remember that our collective power to redefine, to transform and to dream is our greatest strength. I will end here with a quote that I've repeated so much it has become an affirmation to me:

You have to act as if it were possible to radically transform the world. And you have to do it all the time. – Angela Davis

Larissa Kennedy
President, 2020-2022
National Union of Students

Preface A: A love letter to our students

Dear students,

You have what it takes to succeed in your educational endeavours. In today's world it may seem that you have little choice but to go to university, because it's 'just the next thing to do'. You may know exactly where you want to go once you have your hard-earned degree. Whatever your reasons, you *are* capable of getting to the end of university with a qualification and an experience that helps you grow positively. There is plenty of information out there that explains how higher education is failing you and how it has failed those who have gone before you. This book seeks to provide you with some of this information, but also practical steps to change what has been deemed almost inevitable in a system that does not yet understand you, and therefore does not yet understand your needs. Here, you will find a series of affirmations with practical solutions to combat both the psychological and practical limitations placed on us by structural racism. Choose what you need from within these pages and use it as your daily reminder of the fact that you deserve access, positivity and success in higher education at any level.

After each affirmation there is a blank page for you to write your reflections, goals, questions, moments, or even contact information in relation to your learning.

This book does not seek to minimise the difficulty of achieving in a system that is rigged against you. We will talk about some of these challenges. But remember this: the strength we have demonstrated as a people and the strength you continue to demonstrate every day as you show up to the class or community that marginalises and minimises your talent, skill and hard work, will help you achieve your dreams.

Preface B: For those who teach/support higher education students of colour

The [university] can no longer be content to plead that it swims with the social current. When necessary, it is its duty to indicate how the direction of the current should be changed. – Dr Eric Williams

With the 'newfound' awareness of the marginalisation of Black and Brown higher education students in the UK, it is important to consider that old ways of working have proven unsuccessful, and therefore it is time to change them. The conversations around anti-racism and decolonisation have been around for more than half a century, and I believe these will continue for some time. There has still been little change to benefit the students who should profit the most from the awareness of institutional and structural racism in higher education. This book provides a loving spin on this conversation. While I will present facts and information that demonstrate the higher education students of colour in the UK, this book seeks to equip those who care with an understanding of the needs of students beyond the course content.

Research shows evidence of marginalisation in the student of colour population when compared with their White counterparts. There is further evidence suggesting that Black Afro and Caribbean students are marginalised within groupings of students of colour. Asking why this is, what it means and how to fix it is a long journey. Along the way, I hope this book will provide some insight, support and meaningful considerations for all those reading it.

Dissecting cultural impact on education, though a major task, should be done in any environment where success for students of colour is considered. While a series of affirmations, culturally specific student societies, or racially compatible mentorship schemes, won't solve all the issues, they can be an important start. Understanding the similarities and differences within communities of colour will help guide institutions in supporting the learning journey of all students.

Finally, for those who say you love us, our White colleagues, this book is designed to give you some insight. Insight not only into the challenges faced by and the value of our students of colour, but also how you can help build them up despite the difficulties you are often unable to see, identify with, or understand.

This book is written for students, but it will be valuable for you too. Use the language, affirmations and information in this book to meaningfully engage with your students of colour, and provide them with an environment that is conducive to learning.

Why affirmations?

We are going to emancipate ourselves from mental slavery because whilst others might free the body, none but ourselves can free the mind. Mind is your only ruler, sovereign. The man who is not able to develop and use his mind is bound to be the slave of the other man who uses his mind.

– Marcus Garvey

Affirmation #1

I deserve to be here. My ancestors built this place.

You deserve to be here

Britain's economy and cultural heritage remains inextricably tangled with the after effects of slavery, a tangle which we are only beginning to recognise in full. – Museum of London and Docklands

Even if our ancestors did not literally set every brick in place, their suffering likely funded the development of the very streets we walk, the lecture halls and libraries we study in. We can see evidence of this in the names of various slaveholders clearly displayed on the buildings, businesses and streets of this nation. Understanding your birth-right and history will be a lifelong process, but the beginning and end of it has the same message.

There has been much progress by way of access to higher education in recent years, with universities working to ensure there are more opportunities for students of colour to get into university than ever before. Though access has improved, there are still significant awarding, retention and success gaps between students of colour and their peers. This means that while it may be easier to get in, it is often difficult for universities to adequately cater for students of colour within an institution.

Use every resource, person and thing at your disposal to help you understand this journey of university. This means looking for support, and also understanding that even before you set foot on a campus (virtually or in person), you are entitled to the best learning experience that can be offered by your institution. You should feel supported, clear and motivated to succeed. If you don't, remember you are entitled to this.

You deserve to be here.

Notes, reflections, and goals

Decolonisation and anti-racism

Decolonisation has become a much-used word in higher education institutions of late. It is an approach that is about challenging and changing the way that our (people of colour's) history, beliefs and ways of life have been wrongly portrayed. It seeks to intentionally question whether the whats, hows and whys of university studies provide a true picture of a topic, or whether it has been presented in a way that reinforces classist, racist and discriminatory behaviours. These discriminatory behaviours historically came from the presence of European empires across the world that intentionally minimised the cultures of our ancestors and deemed their own the dominant and 'best' cultures.

Anti-racism is what it says on the tin. Racism was a major part of colonialism's success, and so in the effort to decolonise anti-racism is crucial. Anti-racism is a very active and intentional approach that we must take to uproot the historical oppression that still faces people of colour today. Racism can manifest in both systems and processes that work against us, as well as words and actions by individuals who continue to oppress us. Some forms of racism are not obvious, requiring researchers and people like us who have lived experiences of racism to speak up and make change.

As a result of the global conversations taking place about public and hidden acts of racism, Islamophobia and oppression, many universities have adopted new anti-racist or inclusive strategies that focus on equity for students of colour. These documents are often well-written and based on research. The problem with these strategies is they often require whole institution buy-in and change in order to be successful. Nonetheless, these documents (usually accessible online) can give you insight into the support and opportunities available to students of colour at any university.

Practical steps:

1. Most universities have at least one person responsible for supporting anti-racism in the university. Find that person; find out how you can support this work and how they can support you.

2. If one does not exist, start your own anti-racist student society or network that can support you and others like you. Anti-racism is both radical action and listening action. We need our own spaces to share our feelings and experiences. It is ok that these spaces are exclusive to us and do not include White people.

3. Many universities have started the work of decolonisation, whether this is in reading lists, or groups of staff and students who work together to change the way things have been done until now. It is important to be a part of this work and be vocal in these spaces.

4. Hold your lecturers, course team and faculty accountable for being clear about anti-racism policies and how they actively support them.

5. Look at what is said on a university's social media or website. If they are actively talking about anti-racism, inclusivity and decolonising, then this is a good sign. If there is a static page that hasn't changed much, or little mention of this work in their socials, then make sure to ask a lot of questions.

Notes, reflections, and goals

Affirmation #2

There *are* people who understand me here.

Creating a space for you

Be intentional about creating a positive, constructive, and supportive network around yourself. There are many people who desperately want you to succeed.

While the responsibility should remain with the university to fix attainment, awarding, retention and success gaps, the conversation has been going on for (in my opinion) too long without making the changes that need to take place for students of colour to feel just as at home as their White colleagues. This has been found to lead to a sense of non-belonging, where students of colour are unable to effectively assimilate or engage with the learning environment. This has been proven to have a detrimental impact on student success.

Students often feel more connected to their learning at university when they are part of a community outside of the classroom. This includes student societies and mentoring programmes. It is important that you seek out communities of people who have values, experiences and cultures like you. The interpretation of university life and learning in these spaces may make more sense to you and may provide you with a sense of comfort you cannot acquire anywhere else.

There are people who understand me here.

Practical steps to take:

1. Look for, and sign up to, any peer or staff mentoring programmes offered by your university, especially mentoring programmes that partner staff/students of colour with students of colour.

2. Look for any societies you think will meet your needs, both as a student and a person. If none exist, create one.

3. Identify your cultural heritage and ethnicity in as many appropriate places as possible, such as on your student profile/data.

4. Look out for, and sign up to, any special projects, jobs or responsibilities that are designed specifically for students of colour, such as scholarships, or internships.

Notes, reflections, and goals

Affirmation #3

My time is expensive, important and valuable.

Time is not measured by the passing of years but by what one does, what one feels, and what one achieves.

– Jawaharlal Nehru

Finding time for things that matter: time and balance

Find the time for things that matter. Both to you as a person of colour and to you as a student, parent, child, sibling, volunteer, employee or employer, care leaver, whatever your circumstance. Effective time management allows us to create balance in our lives. It also allows us to measure and monitor the areas of our lives that are imbalanced and need to be addressed for us to achieve our goals. Therefore, be aware that time allows us to continuously grow, improve on and understand ourselves. [1]

Conversations around time management at university usually focus on the activities that are required for successful attainment of a degree or qualification. While there are obvious reasons for this focus, there are also a lot of resources available to help guide you. However, less emphasis is placed on the use of free time, as in the time we use for 'non-essential' activities.

Research has found that most students do not use their free time efficiently to keep up with their daily chores, and those who waste their free time are also prone to wasting the valuable time they have for essential activities such as completing assessments. [2,3] People who are motivated and inclined to maintain a strong work/life balance are those who are aware of the importance of free time. [4]

My time is expensive, important and valuable.

Most universities offer students time management training from the start of their programme and throughout. Take advantage of this support. Time management is a crucial skill to develop, not only to help you manage your period of study, but also as a critical skill for professional development and life in general.

Notes, reflections, and goals

Affirmation #4

What I sacrifice today will return to me tomorrow.

[We] should always aim to play the long game. Instant gratification cannot build a legacy.

– Andrena Sawyer

Money management

While the above quote applies to many elements of our lives, in the context of this book it's about money. As a student, you may be entitled to a student loan, grant, scholarship and/or other forms of income that are given to you to support your time studying. Whatever your source of income, it is important to plan financially and use money wisely.

It may be that you have never had to manage large sums of money before, or perhaps you have not had to manage the expenses of studying at university. There can be many unexpected expenses that arise, whether from your course or personal life.

Practical steps to take:

1. Create a budget at the beginning of every year and check in on it every month.

2. Find out what financial support is offered to students at the institution. This could be payment plans, or even cash deposits made for unexpected situations that affect your studies, i.e. funeral expenses, broken laptop.

3. Ask previous students about course costs.

4. Inquire about the reliability and cost of public transport for commuting.

5. Try to avoid making large purchases during your studies, such as a car or large household appliances.

6. Make sure that money for university is just for university. Do not use it to support anything else; the assumption that you will find it somewhere else is rarely true.

Notes, reflections, and goals

Affirmation #5

Do what you must, do what you can, do what you want.

I can achieve what I set out to do today/this week. I can achieve it because I have planned well, and I am motivated. I already have the tools, and when I do not understand, I will ask for help.

Setting goals

Goal setting is a significant component of time and university management. When you don't set appropriate, measurable and achievable goals in life, this can reduce your level of motivation. [5] Setting goals can become very difficult in a new environment and can clash with who you are as a person. Nonetheless, it is still possible to set achievable goals throughout your studies. The ultimate goal of university studies is to complete your degree. Some may go further and say the goal is to become more employable. However, for us, this singular focus on 'completion' may also be to our detriment.

A key component of academic success takes place outside of the standard curriculum and classroom experiences. The traditional view of learning in many of our communities can be quite myopic, often focusing on the completion of work and high grades. However, research has shown that academic success must take into consideration other factors, such as the learning environment, peer engagement and culture. So, in setting your goals, aiming for high grades is great, with a structured and timely approach to completing assignments. But also consider the 'non-academic' goals discussed above, such as creating meaningful networks and organising your free time around activities that you enjoy.

I can achieve what I set out to do today/this week.

Practical steps to take:

1. Making time-bound lists that relate to your academic learning.

2. Asking questions at the start of a course, rather than at the point of submission.

3. Preparing to write draft assessments that can be reviewed by a tutor or colleague.

4. Considering the activities that you wish to complete outside your direct learning, such as exercise, social events, family time.

Notes, reflections, and goals

Affirmation #6:

Today I will be kind to myself and others. I will speak positivity and productivity into my life.

The best fighter is never angry.

– Lao Tzu

Communication versus talking

This book is based on research showing that speaking positively can change your perspective. It can motivate you, and it can motivate other people in your circles. Unfortunately, many of us have grown up surrounded by negative talk. We also continue to consume negativity from our surroundings from places like social media, television and the internet. Sometimes this negativity may have been from those who do not understand our diverse cultures, or those who do not wish to understand. Sometimes it has even come from those who are closest to us. In many ways, you have already begun the process of rejecting some negativity by applying and going to university. Let's continue these positive actions by aiming to speak positively on a daily basis. Do the same for your peers as you may not know what they are going through; your kind words may be the motivation they need to keep going.

I will speak positivity and productivity into my life.

Notes, reflections, and goals

Talking to others

Research has found that people with effective communication skills are better at eliminating conflicts. Individuals who know how to respectfully speak and listen to others are often motivated to develop their interpersonal relationships in society. [6] This is so important. Many students have told me that university can become very isolated and divorced from real life. We explored above how important it is to find and sustain a network at university. This can be a period of great change in your own and your peers' lives. So speak kindly to one another.

Today I will be kind to myself and others.

Conflict management also applies to those in positions of authority in your university experience, including lecturers and other staff. At times, because of the colour of your skin, you may be discriminated against. It is important to recognise when this happens and communicate as effectively as you can, not to escalate the conflict, but to assert your rights. There is always someone at the university who will advocate for you if a situation gets out of control. Check in with your student union, your institutional anti-racist lead and your mentor.

Notes, reflections, and goals

Talking in your language

Along with more melanin in our skin, we also have lots of flavour in our food, colour in our lives, and unique ways of speaking. With our cultural diversity comes diversity in language that is informed by our ancestral languages and the communities we have been raised in. These languages include Patois, Hindi, Igbo, Punjabi, Twi and many others.

You should feel comfortable speaking in your own language, although this may be easier said than done. This is why it's important to find a network and a mentor that allow you to bring your whole self to your university experience. Beyond your own cultural and colloquial languages, at university there is a new language you have to learn: academic language.

Later in the book, I will give some more insight into 'academic language' and how this affects our ability to produce university work that is considered acceptable. Academic language is usually a totally different language from the one we (and by we, I mean anyone) speak on a daily basis. However, being fluent in academic language can go a long way to being perceived as a 'good' and knowledgeable student. Again, this is not the type of education system we want to enforce, but it is the reality for now, and this book is here to help you 'play the game', so we can change the rules in the long run.

Notes, reflections, and goals

Affirmation #7

There are people who understand me here. There are people here who want to see me succeed.

When I walk along with two others, from at least one I will learn.

– Confucius

Find a mentor

#RepresentationMatters is a hashtag that has real meaning and depth for people like us, particularly in settings like higher education where academic success is the goal. In my personal journey, but also in the journeys of many successful students and staff of colour in higher education, I have found that mentorship plays a major role in keeping students at university, and in students being able to achieve success. This is particularly the case when your mentor reflects you – your culture, your language, your background and experiences. Finding a mentor who you can relate to, who understands you and can support you personally and academically will be valuable in this journey of learning.

When you start university, look for teachers, or other staff (librarians, managers) who have experience of UK higher education, but also who have experiences that can enhance your own as a student of colour. Take your time finding someone who communicates with you effectively and respectfully. Be clear that what you need from them is reasonable and set goals to achieve with this person's support. These goals can be both academic and personal, which will help you understand yourself and the world around you.

Notes, reflections, and goals

Affirmation #8

I can learn, I have learned, and I will continue to learn.

Be content with what you have, rejoice in the way things are. When you realise there is nothing lacking, the whole world belongs to you.

− Lao Tzu

Code switching: academic study skills

Code switching is when someone has to change the way they appear or are perceived to make themself understood or more palatable for the environment they are in. Code switching in academic environments is normal for many people of colour, particularly those who have grown up surrounded by a culture that is not White and middle to upper class. You may find yourself code switching most often in your writing and public speaking.

In this next section, we will discuss how to code switch where appropriate. This is because most degrees still require students to present their work in a particular way, in a particular style and language. This language rarely aligns with the language we speak from day to day, and so it is important to know how to speak this language as early as possible in your university experience.

Notes, reflections, and goals

I was made for the library, not the classroom. The classroom was a jail of other people's interests. The library was open, unending, free.

– Ta-Nehisi Coates

Code switching to write: academic writing

Varying based on your course, it is likely that many of your assessments will require you to do some writing. I hope this changes in the future, but for now writing is required.

Writing for university can be very different from any other style of writing you have encountered before. Some subjects are very good at teaching students how to write effectively for success on their course. For example, students studying creative writing and literature are more likely to be taught *how* to write as well as *what* to write. However, some subjects and teachers are less effective at teaching their students how to write, which leaves you with the responsibility of figuring this out.

How to write? Yes, it seems silly when you have likely been writing and typing letters, words and sentences since primary school. At university, academic writing is a method of conveying your thoughts, what you have read, and your analysis of what you have learned in a particular way. In this section, I will not go into the technicality of what academic writing looks like – this information will be available to you when/before you start university. What I do want to share is that ALL universities have a responsibility to provide academic writing support. This is usually through a department providing workshops, tutorials and even in your lessons through your lecturer.

Practical steps to take:

1. At the start of your university journey, seek out this department; they will be more than happy to help you understand what academic writing looks like, and hopefully to help you make it subject-specific. This team may be a part of your school or faculty, or they may be a central team not directly associated with your faculty.

2. Ask your lecturer for examples of what your work should look and sound/read like and try not to feel ashamed to ask questions about words you don't understand.

3. Many universities now have peer tutoring sessions that are a friendly space for you to ask someone more knowledgeable questions about what happened during your lesson. Seek out these sessions and attend.

Notes, reflections, and goals

Reading

Reading is a vital part of your university learning experience. You will encounter information, knowledge and analysis that you most likely have never interacted with before. You will also encounter reading that exposes you to new ideas, thoughts and behaviours. This is one of the most amazing parts of university learning and will be fundamental to your ability to analyse texts and share your own thoughts.

Read what is asked of you.

You will be given reading lists on all your courses. These should provide you with more information and background on the topics of discussion in your lessons. Lately, universities have been learning that reading lists perpetuate ideas and knowledge that come from very White, unrelatable, and at times inaccurate spaces. Many universities are working to correct this by attempting to diversify their reading lists, including authors, countries and topics with wider backgrounds.

Practical steps:

1. No matter how White your reading list is, engage with the resources you have been given. The more you read, the better.

2. Take time to get to know your library. As well as helpful support about how to avoid getting in trouble for academic cheating (plagiarism), they usually have resources that can help you learn more widely about your subject.

3. Make suggestions to your lecturer, course team and faculty about ways the reading list can be changed to be more relevant to you, i.e. does your music resource list include styles such as Soca, or Bangra, and musicians of colour?

4. Find out what people from your cultural heritage/background have to say about the subject. The experiences of people of colour often generate different meanings from those offered as 'good knowledge' in education.

Notes, reflections, and goals

I think therefore, I am.

– René Descartes

Critical thinking

This is a tricky one. You will come across the term 'critical thinking' a lot in your university experience. This is because higher education is designed to support and develop lifelong learners. Universities want to create students who are informed, but also who think for themselves so they can create meaningful change in work and society (well at least that's what I think they should want).

Critical thinking is the ability to see a 'thing', and take all the knowledge you have to challenge, analyse and determine that the 'thing' is indeed a 'thing', or that it is something else.

Let's use an example.

I've been given a reading list. My reading list is made up of predominantly White men, who are European and lived in the 19th century. Critical thinking applied here will show me that, given that reading list, the thoughts and information from these authors are likely to be very biased and only present one view of the topic. Based on what the topic is, this one-sided view is unlikely to be all I need to know to present a good final assessment on my course. Engaging critically would mean seeking out other resources, learning about differing viewpoints on the same topic, and writing an essay that looks at a variety of viewpoints on the topic. Then it means coming to a conclusion in my essay that considers a variety of views and experiences, and therefore is a more realistic representation of the topic.

The example above talks about critical thinking in your subject. Critical thinking is not limited to research within your subject. Using these critical thinking skills will help you to challenge what you are told by lecturers and others in the university. As people of colour, our knowledge, understanding and cultures have been silenced for hundreds of years. For us, critical thinking may mean questioning whether what your lecturers say is true, or accurate. It may mean challenging the resources you are given. All of this should be a part of your university experience. If ever you are marked down for thinking outside the box, don't hesitate to file a complaint to the relevant person.

Notes, reflections, and goals

Affirmation #9

I can learn, I have learned, and I will continue to learn. I won't let my failures define me. I will let my failures teach me.

It is better to submit and get a low mark than not submit at all.

– Melanie-Marie Haywood

Assessment

Assessments are usually conducted as a way of measuring a student's ability to meet the learning outcomes on the module or course.

What are 'learning outcomes'? – These are usually three to five bullet points shared with you at the start of a module. They indicate what a student should know and be able to demonstrate or apply by the end of their learning journey on the module. They usually start with this statement:

By the end of this module, students should be able to...

Assessments are usually formative or summative. Formative assessments are done throughout the module to allow the lecturer to gauge where the students are, but also to provide you with feedback so you know how well you're doing on the course. Effective formative assessments should help you successfully complete your summative assessments. Summative assessments are usually done at the end of a module and are the final stage in assessing your learning across a module. This can be done through an exam, coursework, portfolios or through media and art (in traditional subjects).

Assessments are crucial to your university outcomes and experience. It is the collection of assessment grades that determines your final degree classification. This tends to make students feel that the responsibility lies entirely with them. However, universities have a massive responsibility to ensure that ALL learners are given as much support as necessary to succeed on their course.

Practical steps:

1. Seek out the academic study skills team at your university. They have tutors, workshops and one-to-one sessions to help you understand your assessment(s).

2. If you don't understand anything in your assessment, speak up. Your lecturers want you to submit and are responsible for making sure you do so. It reflects poorly on them if you do not.

3. Please submit something! Most students (over 75%) who submit, pass. If you do not submit, you cannot pass.

Notes, reflections, and goals

Affirmation #10

My words have meaning, and my voice carries weight. No matter how big, or small, my opinions matter and can effect change in my life and in the lives of others.

You can't let your failures define you. You have to let your failures teach you.

– Barack Obama

Share your views on learning experiences

Research over the years has shown that lecturers tend to value the constructive feedback from their students. [7] Research has also shown that student engagement is usually a difficult and nuanced matter and, in particular, students of colour are least likely to ask for help or clarity, or give feedback to their lecturers. [8] Your words can have major implications, not only for your own learning, but for the learning of your colleagues, and all the other Black and Brown students who will attend university after you.

Your feedback could make a marked difference in your classroom learning experiences, but could also go on to change institutional policy, strategy, graduate attributes, and your professional career and development opportunities. It is important that you share your feedback with your lecturers, but also that this feedback is constructive and clear.

Things to consider in giving feedback to your lecturers include:

1. The need for inclusive language in feedback from your lecturer. Define what inclusive is for you as a student of colour and ask your lecturer to consider this.

2. Diversity in assessment – finding ways to allow your culture and learning preferences to be considered in your assessments.

3. The teaching strategies used, and alternative ways to teach the subject or engage with the content that works for students with

your leaning preferences, but also does not create an unachievable workload for your lecturer.

4. Using blended learning approaches to provide flexibility in the learning experience

5. Using a more inclusive and decolonised reading list, or providing one or two new/alternative sources that can be used on the reading list.

Notes, reflections, and goals

Affirmation #11

Remind yourself of all the things that could go right, and not just what can go wrong. There is always another opportunity to change, improve, and do better.

Feedback is a tool for learning

It can be quite daunting to receive individualised feedback on your work. Lecturers and markers all have a unique style, and while most universities have standards for quality on feedback practices, there is still room for some personalisation in the feedback you receive.

It is important that the feedback you receive:

1. Is based on the assessment criteria (also known as a rubric) given to you before you attempted/submitted your work.

2. Is individualised, meaning it is clear the marker has read what you submitted, and the feedback reflects the unique elements of your submission.

3. Feeds forward, so you understand how your submission has done well, and what you should continue doing, but also what needs to change in your future submissions.

Earlier, we established that the language of higher education is often not the language of fluency for the average Black and Brown student, though we cope and adapt. If you find it difficult to understand the feedback you are given, or how your feedback is helpful for your other assignments, extra-curricular learning and academic practice, you should speak to your lecturer or your mentor. You could even ask a trusted colleague or friend to go through the feedback with you and share their perspective. Universities also have free one-to-one tutorials through their study skills or student success programmes. You will be given a personal tutor at the start of your studies, and they can direct you toward someone who can spend time going through your assessments and their feedback with you.

Notes, reflections, and goals

Affirmation #12

I was born to be a changemaker. No matter how big or small, I will make change for the better.

Bibliography

[1] Ağduman, F. (2014). Üniversite öğrencilerinin boş zaman motivasyon ve tatminlerinin incelenmesi (Yayımlanmamış yüksek lisans tezi). Atatürk Üniversitesi, Erzurum.

[2] Hickerson, B. D., & Beggs, B. A. (2007). Leisure time boredom: issues concerning college students. *College Student Journal,* 41, 1036-1044.

[3] Shaikh, B. T., & Deschamps, J. P. (2006). Life in a university residence: issues, concerns and responses. *Education for Health,* 19(1), 43-51.

[4] Ağduman, F. (2014). Üniversite öğrencilerinin boş zaman motivasyon ve tatminlerinin incelenmesi (Yayımlanmamış yüksek lisans tezi). Atatürk Üniversitesi, Erzurum.

[5] Lamb, M. (2017). The motivational dimension of language teaching. *Language teaching, surveys and studies,* 50(3), 301-346.

[6] Oya, T., Manalo, E., & Greenwood, J. (2004). The influence of personality and anxiety on the oral performance of Japanese speakers of English. *Applied Cognitive Psychology,* 18, 841-855.

[7] Floden, J. (2016). The impact of student feedback on teaching in higher education. *Assessment & Evaluation in Higher Education,* 42(7), 1-15.

[8] Royal, K. D., & Singletary, G. T. (2017). Black student participation rates also a concern for educational program assessments. *Journal of National Black Nurses' Association: JNBNA,* 28(2), 40-43.

Lightning Source UK Ltd.
Milton Keynes UK
UKHW020037230822
407663UK00009B/891

9 781999 753092